WINGMEN WARRIORS

Jonathan Bliss

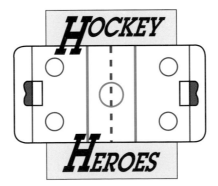

Rourke Book Company, Inc.
Vero Beach, Florida 32964

The Rourke Book Co., Inc.
P.O. Box 3328, Vero Beach, FL 32964

Bliss, Jonathan.
      Wingmen warriors / by Jonathan Bliss.
            p.   cm.—(Hockey heroes)
      Includes bibliographical references (p.) and index.
      ISBN 1-55916-013-6
      1. Hockey players—Juvenile literature. [1. Hockey players.] I. Title.   II. Series.
      GV847.25.B54 1994
      796.962'092'2—dc20
      [B]   93-39507
                                                                   CIP
                                                                    AC

Series Editor: Gregory Lee
Book design and production: The Creative Spark, San Clemente, CA
Cover photograph: Rick Stewart/ALLSPORT

Printed in the USA

Contents

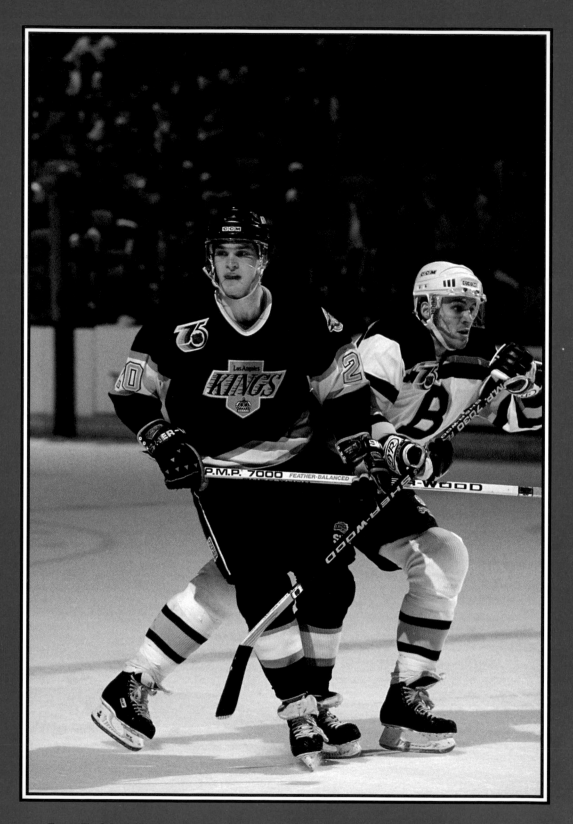

Luc Robitaille is one of the premier forward scorers in the NHL.

The Scoring Machines

On a perfect rush, the center and wings speed down the ice together, entering the zone a split-second after the puck passes the blue line, slipping through the wall of defenders, bearing down on the goalie. They pass the puck back and forth—right wing to center to left wing—until they are within a few feet of the goal crease. Finally the goalie commits and an opening appears. Faster than it seems possible, the puck streaks to a winger's waiting stick and whistles by the helpless goalie into the net. It's a picture-perfect play requiring split-second timing between three members of the line.

Forwards are the ultimate scoring machines in hockey, and the wingers—both

---

Wingmen Trivia

Q: *What player holds the record for the most seasons played in the NHL?*
A: *Gordie Howe, with 26.*

Q: *Who is the oldest person ever to play in the NHL?*
A: *Gordie Howe was 51 years old during his final season.*

Q: *Who holds the record for the most seasons scoring 20 or more goals?*
A: *Gordie Howe, with 22 seasons.*

the right and left wing—provide two-thirds of that punch. Sometimes, when they are all in motion, it is difficult to tell which player is playing which position. They weave and shift and dodge about the ice, always trying to shake their defenseman, fighting for that half-second of freedom which is all they need to get the puck and score.

Hockey is such a fast game. Decisions are made in between heartbeats, and a great player is separated from a merely good one by intuition and a fraction of a second.

Ordinarily, the right wing is positioned to the right of the goalie and the center (as seen from the opposite end of the ice). Because he is on the right side of the crease he usually shoots righthanded. The left wing occupies the left side of the zone, to the left of the goalie and the center. He generally shoots lefthanded.

There are four types of shots wingers will employ during the course of a game: the slapshot, the wristshot, the backhander, and the deflection. The slapshot is the hardest of the four. It takes a high backswing followed by a powerful swing downward. Ideally, the flat of the stick meets the puck at its lowest point and propels the puck toward the net at speeds exceeding 100 miles an hour. Think of it as a golf swing on ice. The wristshot is more subtle and more difficult to anticipate. The player merely flicks his wrist and lifts the puck toward the net. The backhander is a variation on the wristshot: The player shifts the puck to the backside of his hockey blade and flips the puck up into the goal. It is commonly used when the player has the puck on the "wrong" side of his stick; for example, when a righthanded player has the puck on the left side of his body.

The deflection is the most difficult shot to set up. The player places the blade of his stick in the path of a shot already taken by another player, redirecting the shot. The great shooters can redirect a slapshot into any corner of the net with only a slight twist of their stick blade.

Shooting is what the winger is all about, and Russian-born star Sergei Makarov is one great shooter for the Calgary Flames.

Hockey has always been a hard game in which to score. Name almost any other sport and you will see more scoring. Basketball, baseball, football—they all score points in bunches. Only soccer comes close to hockey in scoreboard stinginess. Until recently, the normal hockey game ended in a 3-2 or a 2-1 score (when it didn't end in a tie). Even today, with its comparatively high-scoring games, a normal game of hockey is a 5-4 or 6-5 affair. Unless you are dealing with a real powerhouse, few teams will score more than five or six points during a game. You will almost never see a team score 10 or more goals in a game.

The winger must score if his team is to win. For this reason, the success or failure of a winger is

Wingers are the offensive thrust of a hockey team, and when they're on a roll, even the referee better stay out of their way!

measured by the number of points he has scored during the course of a regular or playoff season—either by scoring a goal or assisting in the score of a goal.

Of course, it is necessary for the winger to fall back on defense, too, doing his part to keep the opposing forwards from the front of the net. But his primary job is to break out a split-second after the puck has been captured by a member of his team, skate like crazy for the opposite end, be ready for a pass when it comes while remaining onside, cross the opponent's blue line after the puck has, and shoot the puck at the first opportunity. This is difficult, to say the least, but back in the 1870s when hockey was just becoming popular, it was even more difficult. For one thing, there was no forward passing; hockey players were not allowed to pass the puck forward, only sideways. Players passed whenever they met resistance, which was all the time, since there was no rule prohibiting defensemen from staying in their own zone.

Shooting is only one of the winger's talents. He must be able to move easily with the puck, which means he must be equally proficient at passing and stickhandling. He must also be able to move well without the puck—a far more difficult task requiring considerable speed and great conditioning. It helps if he can take a hit, too, or a crosscheck. Since the winger handles the puck more than the other players on the ice, he inevitably attracts more of the defensemen's attention. Because he is the first line of defense, a forward must also know how to block, pokecheck, tackle, and dish it out when necessary.

The players who can do all of these things are NHL material. Those few who can do them truly well, are the immortals of the game. Here, then, are the stories and statistics behind some of the great wingers in hockey history.

Jari Kurri is a new breed of winger. Many Hall of Famers never dreamed of scoring as many goals per season as Kurri does routinely.

The First Great Wingers

The first documented hockey game took place on a frozen lake at McGill University in Montreal, Canada—a game for college football and lacrosse players keeping fit while waiting for spring to come. That was March 3, 1875. The game quickly gained favor and was soon being played by both men and women alike—brandishing crooked sticks, wearing long fur coats, playing keepaway with a flat rubber disc.

Within two decades the game was popular enough to support professional players and numerous leagues throughout Canada and the United States. People paid good money to see their favorite players. Then as now, most of their favorites were on the front line.

Jimmy Gardner was one of the first star right wingers in

the game. He was a member of two great teams during the early years of hockey: the Montreal Hockey Club and the Montreal Wanderers. He won the Stanley Cup with the Montreal Hockey Club in 1902 after a heroic effort against the Winnipeg Victorias, the best team of that era. Gardner's play, along with that of Dickie Boon and several other future Hall-of-Famers, earned the team their nickname, "Little Men of Iron." In 1910, he helped the Wanderers win the Stanley Cup. He went to the west coast to play for New Westminster in 1911, but returned east to play for the Montreal Canadiens in 1915.

Harry Cameron was one of the game's first innovators. Over a 14-year career in three major hockey leagues Cameron scored 171 goals in 312 games. Cameron played on three Stanley Cup champions based in Toronto: the 1914 Torontos, the 1918 Arenas, and the 1922 Pats. He is best remembered as the first player to curve his shots without modifying his stick. He accomplished this by adding "English" to the puck—slapping the puck in such a way that it turned rapidly as it came at the unhappy goalie. The curved shot dips unexpectedly just like a "knuckler" pitch in baseball.

Billy Gilmour was the talented right wing for the Ottawa Silver Seven at the turn of the century. He won three consecutive Stanley Cups with that team (1903 to 1905). Gilmour then showed his worth by winning a fourth Stanley Cup in 1909 playing for the Ottawa Senators. He finished the season with 11 goals in 11 games.

Arthur Farrell was another of the game's great innovators. He joined the Montreal Shamrocks in 1897 and played with them through the 1901 playoffs, collecting two Stanley Cups along the way. On March 2, 1901, Farrell had the best game of his career when he scored five goals against the Quebec Bulldogs! But

Farrell is remembered best for his stylish playmaking. Previously, hockey had been pretty much an individual's game, but Farrell made team-play popular.

Individual Excellence

Harry "Punch" Broadbent still holds the record for scoring in the most consecutive games. He accomplished this feat during the 1921-22 season when the talented right winger scored goals in 16 straight games for the Montreal Maroons. He started his professional hockey career at the age of 16, playing for Ottawa in the old National Hockey Association in 1912. In his first year with the Senators he scored 21 goals in 24 games. Two seasons later he scored 24 goals. In 1921-22, he scored an amazing 32 goals to lead the league. He played for several teams and won four Stanley Cups—three at Ottawa and one more with the Maroons—before retiring in 1930. Broadbent came by his nickname honestly. He was as good with his elbows and fists as he was with his stick, leading the league one season in both goals and penalty minutes.

Hockey oldtimers remember Thomas Neil Phillips with particular fondness as the best player of his day. Phillips played left wing for McGill before joining the Montreal Triple A club in 1902. In 1906-07, he starred for the Kenora Thistles when they won the Stanley Cup, scoring all four goals in the first game of the series. Playing for the Ottawa Senators in 1907-08, Phillips was shifted to right winger, but it only seemed to improve his game: In 10 games he scored 26 goals! Phillips had everything a good winger should have: great speed, a powerful shot, and peerless stickhandling. Sadly, he died in 1923 at the age of 43.

Gordon Roberts was one of hockey's greatest left wingers—in his spare time. While establishing himself as one of the Montreal Wanderers' greatest stars, he was also attending medical school at McGill University. He entered McGill in 1911 and played six seasons with the Wanderers. He had a heavy shot that star goalie Clint Benedict claimed would curve as a result of Roberts' powerful wrist action. He earned his medical degree in 1916 and left for the west coast where he practiced medicine while continuing to play. He joined the Vancouver Millionaires in 1917 and scored 43 goals in only 23 games, an all-time PCHA record. He retired in 1921 to take up full-time medical practice.

Aurel Joliat was called the "Mighty Atom" and the "Little Giant" because of his diminutive size combined with his prolific scoring. Joliat joined Montreal in 1922 when the Canadiens traded for him in exchange for the great centerman Newsy Lalonde. Aurel did better than fill Lalonde's shoes, he soon became one of the greatest left wingers of all time, playing the next 16 seasons with Montreal. Barely 135 pounds, Joliat was able to elude bigger, stronger players through cunning and superior speed. When he matched up with Bill Boucher and the legendary Howie Morenz in 1923, it created one of the most potent offensive lines in hockey history. Joliat played on three Stanley Cup-winning teams—1924, 1930, and 1931—and won the Hart Trophy in 1934 for the league's most valuable player. In 654 games, Joliat scored 270 goals and 190 assists. In 54 playoff games, he tallied 14 goals and 19 assists.

Conacher and Busher Jackson

Charlie Conacher was big and powerful, with a heavy shot from the right wing that became familiar to every goalie in the NHL. Conacher joined the Maple Leafs at the end of the 1928-29 season after his amateur team, the Toronto Marlboros, had won the Memorial Cup. From the outset, Conacher was at home in the NHL.

One of the early legends of the right wing: Charlie Conacher.

He was a shifty skater, a good stickhandler, and was difficult to stop (especially around the net). He was like a shark sniffing blood; Conacher was a terror on offense and began to show it in 1930-31 when he scored 31 goals and racked up 43 points to rank third among leading scorers in the league.

The following year, Conacher helped the Leafs win the Stanley Cup. Paired with future Hall-of-Famers Harvey Jackson and Joe Primeau, Conacher went on to become a sharpshooter in the NHL. He won the Art Ross Trophy twice, awarded to the highest-scoring NHL player over the course of a season. During the 1933-34 and 1934-35 seasons he scored 52 and 57 points respectively, and was the top goal scorer in the league four consecutive times (1932 to 1936). Conacher was traded to Detroit in 1937 where he played for one year before moving on to the New York Americans. He played with New York until 1941 when he retired. For his career, Conacher scored 225 goals and 173 assists in 12 NHL seasons. He also collected 17 goals and 18 assists in 49 playoff games.

Harvey "Busher" Jackson was the left wing for Toronto's Conacher-Primeau-Jackson line (nicknamed the "Kid Line") that terrorized the league while collecting one Stanley Cup and three championships. Jackson joined the Leafs in 1930 at the ripe age of 19. In 1933, he led the league in scoring with 28 goals and 25 assists and was named to the NHL All-Star team on five occasions. The Kid Line finally broke up after five years when Conacher was brought down by injuries and Primeau retired.

In 1939, Jackson injured his shoulder while playing against Boston during the Stanley Cup finals. He was traded the next year to the New York Americans where he was reunited with Charlie Conacher. In 1942, he went to the Bruins where he closed out his career two years later. In 633 NHL games, Busher Jackson collected 241 goals and 234 assists. In playoff competition, he compiled 18 goals and 12 assists in 72 games.

Over the years, the National Hockey League has modified the rules to help increase scoring and make the game even more exciting. In 1934, the NHL added to the rule book a penalty that remains one of the most exciting plays in hockey: the penalty shot. This shot is the ultimate test of just what a good offensive player can do. The penalty shot is only awarded a handful of times every season, and has only occurred 27 times in the entire history of the Stanley Cup playoffs (resulting in goals only 10 times). The penalty shot is awarded for tripping a player who has a clear breakaway, or for throwing a stick at the puck to prevent a shot on goal. The penalty is an unobstructed rush by one player against the opposition goalie without interference from any other player. In the hands of a crack shooter, this play usually ends in a score—unless the goalie is very hot. Nothing can match watching a great winger face a great goalie!

"The Rocket"—Maurice Richard—was one of the most imposing scorers in hockey history.

The Wings of Eagles

By the mid-1940s, the game of hockey had undergone a face lift. The predominant league, the NHL, was playing a 60-game regular season schedule with each game consisting of three 20-minute periods. Forward passing was a reality, and there were now three lines on the ice—two blue lines and a red midline—with more liberal offsides rules to speed up play. There was also an overtime period added in the event of a tie score at the end of regulation. (The overtime period was originally 10 minutes long but was later changed to five minutes.) If neither team scored at the end of overtime, then the game was declared a tie.

The NHL also assigned one referee and two linesmen to each game, and amended the rule book to include more penalties. This meant there would be more penalties called, and that meant more power plays and more chances to score. These changes made hockey a more offensive and exciting game than ever.

The NHL did a lot of things to speed up the game and make it higher scoring. What they failed to do was increase the size of the league. The "solid six" still ruled the league: Boston, Detroit, Chicago, Montreal, Toronto, and New York. Despite the lack of teams, there was no lack of great players, particularly great wingers. In fact, the late 1940s and 1950s saw the emergence of several wingers who would become hockey's greatest stars.

Rocket Richard

Without a doubt, Maurice Richard was one of the greatest players in hockey history. During his career, "The Rocket" collected more offensive records than anyone in the league except Gordie Howe and Wayne Gretzky (the two men with whom he is most often compared). All-Star goaltender Glenn Hall once said of Richard: "What I remember most about the Rocket were his eyes. When he came flying toward you with the puck on his stick, his eyes were all lit up, flashing and gleaming like a pinball machine. It was terrifying."

Richard was lightning quick. He hustled constantly on the ice, digging pucks out of the corner or picking up the puck in his own end. He also had great stick control. He played right wing, but was utterly unorthodox because he had a lefthanded shot. Not that it really mattered to The Rocket: he was a switch-hitter, equally at home slapping the puck with either hand.

Richard was also physically strong. He simply bowled over any defenseman in his path. Hall of Fame referee Bill Chadwick once said of Richard, "He was the greatest scorer I ever saw from the blue line in. And his strength was amazing. I saw him carry defensemen on his back right up to the goal mouth and score."

Richard's 1944-45 season was unreal. He streaked through the 50-game schedule at an incredible goal-per-game clip, scoring an unheard-of 50 goals, including 15 goals in one nine-game stretch. Ten times during the season he scored two or more goals in a game. No one would ever score 50 goals in a 50-game season again. He was named to the league's All-Star team 14 times.

When at last Richard hung up his skates in 1960, he had been on eight Stanley Cup-winning teams and scored a career 544 goals. The NHL waived its usual three-year waiting period, inducting The Rocket into the Hall of Fame one month after his retirement. The honor was never better deserved.

Ted Lindsay

Pound for pound, Ted Lindsay was one of the best hockey players ever. At 5-feet, 8-inches and 160 pounds, most opponents were taller and heavier than this left winger, but none of them were any tougher. He wore the scars of his NHL battles with pride—more than 400 stitches worth of walls, fists, pucks, and sticks recorded on his face alone. But despite the scar tissue, Lindsay was beautiful to watch on the ice.

Lindsay joined the Detroit Red Wings in 1944, skating with right wing Gordie Howe and center Sid Abel to form the legendary "Production Line" that set all records for goals and assists through the late 1940s and early '50s. Lindsay and the Production Line led the Red Wings to eight regular season league titles (including seven in a row) and four Stanley Cup championships between 1950 and 1955. Lindsay had a string of great offensive years with the Red Wings, but perhaps his best was 1949-50 when he led the league in scoring with 23 goals and 55 assists for 78 points. Lindsay saved his greatest heroics for the playoff finals when his team was behind in the series 3-2, and behind in the game 4-3 to the Rangers. Lindsay tied the score with minutes to play in the third period. Sid Abel came through with the clincher, and Detroit went on to defeat New York 4-3 for the Stanley Cup.

Gordie Howe

Ted Lindsay's partner on right wing was a soft-spoken man with a broad smile and an easygoing manner. Where Lindsay was ferocious, Howe was

No hockey player has surpassed the endurance and consistent quality of Gordie Howe.

gentlemanly. Where Lindsay clobbered anything that moved, Howe merely bumped politely. He was the third man on the Red Wings' Production Line of Lindsay and Abel. At six-feet and 205 pounds he was far from an ominous presence. But no other player in history (with the possible exception of Wayne Gretzky) was as brilliant at the game as Gordie Howe. Jean Beliveau, another star and one of Howe's fiercest rivals, maintained that "Gordie Howe is the best hockey player I have ever seen."

Why was Gordie Howe so good? As a skater, he was as graceful as a swan. He made difficult moves look effortless. Attempts to separate Howe from the puck always seemed to fail. He had arms that would be the envy of any octopus—tentacles that could haul in a puck from six feet away and then shoot at the net in a single motion. Howe could thread the puck through the tiniest openings. Along with his strength came incredible durability: three decades of pounding without any sign of wear.

Gordie Howe was born in 1928 in Floral, Saskatchewan. He joined the Detroit Red Wings for the 1946-47 season when he was 18 years old, but he did not immediately burn up the league. The real beginning of the Howe legend was 1947-48 when the Red Wings first assembled the Production Line of Sid Abel (center), Ted Lindsay (left wing) and Howe (right wing). It produced handsomely in its first year with 63 goals, leading Detroit into the Stanley Cup finals against Toronto.

In 1949-50, the Production Line was unstoppable. Howe finished third in the scoring race with 68 points. Then, in the playoffs, Howe collided with Toronto's Ted Kennedy and crashed head-on into the boards. Rushed to the hospital, he hovered between life and death while surgeons operated to relieve pressure on his brain. He recovered, and came back to lead the Red Wings to four Stanley Cups over the next six years.

Howe became a fixture at the top of the hockey world. He won the Hart Trophy as the league's MVP an incredible six times in two decades. His best offensive year was 1952-53, when he had 49 goals and 46 assists for 95 points (a record at the time). In his 19th season in the league, Howe broke the all-time record for career goals when he passed Maurice Richard's mark of 544 goals and kept right on going.

Howe ended his 25-year career with the Red Wings in 1971. But Howe wasn't finished. After two years of retirement, Howe returned to play with his sons, Marty and Mark, for the WHA's Houston Astros. Although he was in his late forties, Howe was still a legitimate all-star, posting seasons of 96, 99, 100, and 102 points. When the Hartford Whalers joined the NHL in 1979, Howe played one final season, appearing in the 1980 All-Star game (his 21st appearance). He was 51 years old.

Canadien Wingers

Dickie Moore was one pillar of the Montreal Canadiens' greatest dynasty. The hard-working left winger was called up by the Canadiens during the 1951-52 season, and played with Montreal until his retirement in 1963. Plagued throughout his NHL career by injuries, he nevertheless led the NHL in scoring twice: in 1958 (36 goals, 48 assists) and 1959 when he broke Gordie Howe's single-season scoring mark of 95 points by scoring 96. Moore helped the Canadiens clinch six Stanley Cups in eight years, including a record five in a row. His career stats reflect his digging style: in 719 games, Moore compiled 261 goals and 347 assists.

Skating with Dickie Moore was Bernie "Boom Boom" Geoffrion, a ferocious bull of a man who terrorized defensemen. Geoffrion joined the Canadiens in 1951 and promptly scored eight goals in 18 games. He finished out the season in such style that the league awarded him the Calder Trophy for the best rookie. Geoffrion went on to score 393 NHL goals before retiring in 1968. He won the Hart Trophy as MVP when he became only the second man to score 50 goals in a season.

Yvan Cournoyer was a stalwart member of the Canadien dynasties of the 1960s and '70s, proving time and again that he could hold his own against anyone in the league. He was a scrapper, working hard for pucks in the corners, and a fighter when the situation called for it. His greatest asset was his speed; he only needed two or three steps before defenders were forced to backpedal madly.

One big reason for the Montreal Canadiens' success during the 1950s was their hard-working left winger, Dickie Moore.

By the time he retired in 1979, the speedy right winger had collected 428 goals and 435 assists in 16 seasons with the Canadiens.

Rod Gilbert

Rod Gilbert starred as a right winger in the NHL despite numerous career-threatening injuries. He once suffered a broken back, and nearly lost his left leg while in surgery. Doctors once told him he'd never skate again. They were wrong. During 18 seasons with the New York

Alex Delvecchio was only the second player to ever play more than 20 seasons with the same team. His skills helped Detroit win three Stanley Cups.

Rangers, Gilbert set or equalled 20 team scoring records. When he retired in 1977 he trailed only Gordie Howe in total points. His career numbers were 406 goals and 615 assists in 1,065 games, plus 34 goals and 33 assists in 79 playoff appearances. Not bad for a guy who was once told he'd never be able to skate again!

Bobby Hull

They called him the "Golden Jet" because of his blonde good looks, his speed, and—most of all—the rocket shot that inevitably came at the end of an up-ice rush. Bobby Hull was not the first man to take a slapshot, he was merely the best who ever did it.

Bobby Hull had the most talent of anyone in the game. He had a burly chest, trunk-sized legs, weightlifter arms—and still he was fast! He was the fastest skater in the league at the time (28.3 mph with the puck, 29.7 mph without it). Hull's booming slapshots reached more than 118 mph. No defenseman in his right mind would throw himself in front of a Hull slapshot. Goalies dreaded Hull's screamers. Not that many of them had a chance to actually stop a Hull shot. Hull's shot was not only hard and fast, it was also unerring. On average, 40 shots got by rival goalies each year during the 16 seasons Hull played in the NHL.

Hull joined the Chicago Black Hawks in 1957 as a left winger. In the 1961-62 season, Hull became the first player to score more than 50 goals, slamming 54 home. By 1968-69, Hull had increased that mark to 58 goals in a season. In his first 15 years in the league, Hull collected 604 goals, won three scoring championships, and played left wing on 10 All-Star teams. He had also won the Hart Trophy for the NHL's Most Valuable Player twice, the Lady Byng once, and the Lester Patrick Trophy for contributions to hockey in the U.S. once. He became the league's first $100,000-a-year player.

The fleet Bobby Hull and his fearsome slapshot dominated NHL hockey in the 1960s and '70s.

Was Hull worth all this cash to the Black Hawks? Without a doubt. Almost singlehandedly, Hull transformed Chicago from a money-losing venture to a big moneymaker. Along the way, he brought the Black Hawks respectability, leading them to a league championship and a Stanley Cup. In every sense of the word, Bobby Hull was the franchise.

In 1972, Hull accepted a $1 million offer from the World Hockey Association to play for the Winnipeg Jets. In so doing, Hull became one of the pioneers in the new league. Despite missing the first 15 games of the season, Hull scored 50 goals for the sixth time in his career. Hull enjoyed his greatest season in 1974-75 when he scored a phenomenal 77 goals in 78 games for a total of 142 points.

Hull retired in 1980 at the age of 41. He was the

highest-scoring left wing in history with 1,018 goals and 2,017 assists. In 119 playoff games, Hull scored 62 goals and 67 assists. As Stan Mikita, the brilliant Black Hawks' center said: "To say that Bobby was a great hockey player...he was all of that, of course. But the thing I admired about him was the way he handled people. He always enjoyed signing autographs for fans and was a genuine nice guy."

Frank Mahovlich

Despite a brilliant career, Frank Mahovlich was one of the quietest and most private men to play the game. He was a superstar from the moment he broke into the league with Toronto. He won the Calder Trophy as the outstanding rookie in 1958. He helped the Maple Leafs clinch four Stanley Cups before being traded to Detroit, where he played on one of the league's top lines with Alex Delvecchio and Gordie Howe. The "Big M" played three seasons with the Red Wings before being traded to Montreal where his swooping, graceful style helped the Canadiens win two more Stanley Cups. He played four more years in the WHA before retiring at the end of the 1978 season.

Mahovlich retired at the end of the 1974 season, having scored 533 goals and 1,103 total points in 1,181 regular-season games (18 seasons). His NHL playoff record included 51 goals and 67 assists for 118 points in 137 games and six Stanley Cups.

John Bucyk

John Bucyk played left wing for one of the most productive lines of all times—the Boston Bruin's Esposito-Bucyk-Hodge line—that intimidated and infuriated opponents for most of the 1970s. Bucyk was near the top of the league's scorers for a decade starting in 1967. His most brilliant year was 1970-71 when he scored 51 goals and 65 assists in finishing third in the league. "Chief" was also a member of two Stanley Cup winners in Boston (1970 and 1972) and was selected for two All-Star teams. He also won the Lady Byng Trophy for outstanding sportsmanship in the league twice. He retired after the 1977-78 season having scored 556 goals and 813 assists in 1,540 games—all but two of them with Boston.

Guy Lafleur

He was called "The Flower" by his adoring fans not just because that was the English translation of his last name but because of his graceful skating style and dramatic play. This talented right winger was singled out as the next great hockey sensation when he tore up the junior leagues, scoring an amazing 209 points in his final season for Quebec City. The Canadiens claimed him in the 1971 Amateur Draft, but Lafleur did not bloom overnight. It took some time for him to fulfill the expectations of the Montreal fans who crowded into the Montreal Forum to watch him. Lafleur had all the moves: superior speed, a hard accurate shot, and great stickhandling abilities. But it took a while for fans to see that Lafleur had something else as well. The right winger was one of the most creative players of his day. The normal rush up-ice was not enough for him. He had to improvise, passing behind his back to a streaking centerman, or turning back on himself, passing the puck to himself through the opposing player's legs. The crowd had never seen a player like this. Lafleur was exciting. The longer the Montreal fans watched, the more they liked what they saw.

Lafleur's potential was fulfilled in 1974-75 when he embarked on his first of six consecutive 50-goal seasons. During these years, he was consistently the All-Star selection at right wing, won the Art Ross Trophy as scoring champ three times, and the Hart

*Montreal's Guy Lafleur is best remembered for his remarkable
skating and puck handling.*

Trophy for the best player in the league twice. The
results were not surprising: The Canadiens took four
consecutive Stanley Cups from 1976 through 1979. When
he finally retired at the end of the 1984-85 season, Lafleur
had compiled 518 goals and 728 assists in 961 career
games. In playoff competition he had 57 goals and 76
assists in only 124 games resulting in five Stanley Cups.

Mike Bossy

There may have been faster players in the league,
better passers and tough fighters, but no one ever came
close to Mike Bossy when it came to shooting. Bossy was
a pure shooter. He would set up in the right face-off
circle, 10 or 15 feet away from the rival goalie, cruising
into position, his stick poised. At some point one of his
teammates would deliver the puck. What happened next

In his 10-year career Mike Bossy scored 573 goals and 553 assists in only 752 games—more than one point per game.

usually required a slow-motion replay to see clearly. It was like a cobra striking. One moment the puck would be in front of him, the next it was in the net. No one usually saw Bossy hit the puck, yet it magically passed the goalie.

Bossy's entrance into the league was quiet, selected 15th overall in the 1977 draft by the New York Islanders. His first year, Bossy scored a record 53 goals and won the Calder Trophy as the league's best rookie. It was only the beginning. For the next nine consecutive seasons, Bossy would score 50 goals or better, in five of them scoring 60 or better! No one had ever come close to such figures—not Hull, not Howe, not Richard. He was selected to the All-Star team eight times, and helped the Islanders win four consecutive Stanley Cups.

As time went on, the pure shooter became a great passer and playmaker. But he never fought unless he had to. "I didn't fight because I thought fighting was senseless," he said. In this, Bossy agreed with many other players in the league who wanted to see the sport of hockey cleaned up, to lose its image as "boxing on ice."

The secret of his great shotmaking was the speed of his release. Bossy was the master of the "one-timer." He had the remarkable ability to catch and fire the puck in the same motion. But there was something else besides the speed: It was his unfailing aim. Somehow, despite the fact that the puck barely touched his stick, he could direct it anywhere within the radius of that net.

At the beginning of training camp in 1986 he bent over to catch his breath and, when he straightened up, something in his back snapped. No matter how much physical therapy he got, no matter how much he nursed it, the back never got better. In 1987-88, after a year off for rehabilitation, Bossy had the only sub-50-goal season in his career. He sat out the following year, but it did no good. Bossy was forced to retire when he was only 31 years old.

One of the stars of the great Edmonton Oilers' 1980s dynasty, and still going strong: Jari Kurri.

Fast Forwards

Each new superstar that comes along raises the standard of excellence a little higher. The 40-goal scorers of the 1940s never thought it was possible for anyone to score 50 goals in a season. Mike Bossy made it seem almost commonplace, raising the ante to 60 goals a year or higher. Wingers were no longer the loyal right and left hand of the center, they were often the powerhouses that made the whole team run. More foreign stars were finding their way to the NHL, like Swedish defenseman Borje Salming who became the Maple Leafs all-time assist leader in 17 seasons.

Along with more European players came a style of hockey that found its greatest expression in the Edmonton Oilers of the 1980s. The Oilers specialized in speed, stickhandling, and passing. They often threw all five men into the opponent's zone, ignoring the tradition of keeping two men back. The defensemen on the Oilers were as much a part of the charge as the forwards.

The wingmen of today are some of the most gifted ever to play the game. Some combine the skill of a Maurice Richard with the sharpshooting of a Mike Bossy, the endurance of a Gordie Howe, and the muscle of a Bobby Hull. Here are but a few of the remarkable wingmen who play the game today.

Jari Kurri

Finnish import Jari Kurri was instrumental on all five of Edmonton's Stanley Cup-winning teams. He came to Edmonton at the beginning of the 1980-81 season after three years with Jokerit of the Finnish League. Kurri went about the task of dismantling every team he faced. His first year in the NHL he scored 32 goals and 43 assists in 75 games. Kurri just kept getting better: 45 goals and 104 points in 1982-83; 52 goals and 113 points in 1983-84; 71 goals and 135 points in 1984-85; 68 goals (league best) and 131 points in 1985-86; 54 goals and 108 points in 1986-87. If it hadn't been for Wayne Gretzky, Kurri would have placed first in goals, assists, and total points five years in a row.

It was in the playoffs that Kurri often shone the brightest. A big game player, Kurri led the playoffs in goals in four years. There always seemed to be a direct correlation between Kurri's success in the playoffs and an Oilers' Stanley Cup victory. His most formidable talent is his extraordinary shot from the faceoff circle. No player, perhaps not even Mike Bossy, has had a shot as quick and accurate as Kurri's.

Equally as impressive, however, was Kurri's defensive prowess. In an offensive position—and on a team not known for its defense—Kurri was one of the best. He is frequently near the top of the Plus/Minus stats and has been cited as one of the best defensive forwards in the league.

After playing in Milan, Italy, for one year, Kurri was lured back to the States to play for the L.A. Kings alongside his old linemate Wayne Gretzky. In the 1993 playoffs, he rang up nine goals and 13 assists. Once again, there seemed to be a direct connection between Kurri's success and his team's success. This time it led to the Stanley Cup finals.

Every season Brett Hull proves that he has the same talent as his famous father Bobby.

Brett Hull

"Like father, like son." The Golden Jet of the 1960s—Bobby Hull—gave rise to The Golden Brett of the 1990s. Is the son really as good as the father? You better believe it. Brett Hull plays right wing while his old man played left, but otherwise, the physique and the slapshot still look frighteningly familiar. If anything, Brett can skate even better than his father and hold his own just as well.

The Calgary Flames couldn't figure out what to do with this young rookie, even after he scored 26 goals and 24 assists in only 52 games. They traded him to the St. Louis Blues, to their everlasting shame. Hull finished the 1987-88 season in St. Louis and proved important in revitalizing that franchise.

Hull's scoring accelerated to warp speed in 1988-89 when he scored 41 goals and 43 assists in leading St. Louis to a second-place finish in the Norris Division. He collected his first of four All-Star selections. The following year, Hull set the right wing record for most goals in a season when he scored 72, breaking Jari Kurri's mark by one. Hull shattered all records the next year (including his own) by scoring 86 goals and 45 assists. Only Wayne Gretzky ever scored that many goals. Hull was deluged with awards, including the league's MVP.

Brett Hull has established himself as a superstar of the highest calibre. A friendly, unassuming man, he has also managed to deal with his superstardom, remaining one of the truly nice people in the game.

Luc Robitaille

As he comes down the ice pushing the puck in front of him, the crowd erupts in a thundering "Luuuuuuuc!" Lucky Luc Robitaille is on the break again. Robitaille, like Brett Hull, has not let fame go to his head.

In 1986, this Quebec Major Junior Hockey League star was snapped up by the Los Angeles Kings who were desperately in need of a star to replace Marcel Dionne. Robitaille came through, scoring 45 goals and 39 assists in winning the Calder Trophy as the league's outstanding rookie. He is also a six-time All-Star.

During only his second year in the league, Robitaille broke the 100-point mark for the first of six times (so far), as he scored 53 goals and 58 assists. A remarkable shooter from anywhere on the ice, Robitaille is best around the net, poking in rebounds, or wristing shots past a sprawling goalie. Like many of the great players, he has a "nose" for the puck and has developed into a fine passer. Still young, Robitaille is a good bet to only add to his point-scoring exploits in the years to come.

Only a player like Luc Robitaille could consider a 98-point season to be below average.

Motivators

Steve Larmer is at the heart of the Chicago Black Hawks. For the last 10 years, Larmer has played every game of the regular season for Chicago, establishing himself as one of the premier right wings in the league. In his first full season with the Black Hawks he not only scored 43 goals and 47 assists, he also helped raise Chicago from fourth place in the Norris Division to first. For this and other contributions, Larmer was awarded the Calder Trophy as the league's outstanding rookie.

Larmer has three times scored 90 or more points, with his high coming in 1990-91 when he scored 43 goals and 57 assists for 101 points. But Larmer's greatest contribution comes in his leadership. He has taken the Black Hawks to the conference finals four times and the Stanley Cup finals once (1991-92), bringing excitement back to a franchise that has suffered through 31 years since its last Stanley Cup winner.

Sometimes a player is just made for a particular team. Such was the case with Cam Neely, the right winger who came up with the Vancouver Canucks in 1983. Neely didn't play badly for the Canucks, he just wasn't what they wanted. So they traded him to Boston.

From the moment he skated into Boston Garden, it was love. In 1986-87, Neely scored 36 goals and 36 assists. The next year, he rang up 42 goals and 27 assists. More importantly, he led the Bruins into the Stanley Cup finals—their first appearance in a decade. Two years later, Neely struck again, this time for 55 goals (the most since the glory days of Phil Esposito) and 37 assists as he once again led the Bruins into the Stanley Cup finals. He contributed 12 goals and 16 assists in only 21 games.

Michel Goulet is an extraordinarily talented left winger who has enjoyed a string of great years with Quebec and Chicago. He came into the league in 1979 and almost immediately established himself as one of the league's best shooters. Goulet's two best years were 1982-83 when he scored 57 goals and 48 assists, and 1983-84 when he scored 56 goals and 65 assists. Goulet frequently toiled in obscurity while other left wingers with less talent received greater media attention because they played on better teams. Yet Goulet is among the top five wingers in career goals, assists, and points.

Dave Taylor has been the jewel in the L.A. Kings' crown since 1977. Before there was Gretzky, before there was Kurri or Robitaille or Sandstrom, Dave Taylor was The Man in L.A. This right winger tyrannized the league alongside center Marcel Dionne and left wing

Cam Neely is a one-man scoring machine, contributing 20 points in just 19 playoff games during the 1990-91 season.

Charlie Simmer. His best year came in 1980-81 when he scored 47 goals and 65 assists for 112 points. In 1991, he was awarded both the King Clancy Memorial Trophy and the Bill Masterton Memorial Trophy as the athlete contributing the most to hockey.

After 15 seasons in the same town, most observers probably thought Taylor was out of moves. Wrong again. In fact, Taylor was a unifying force in the Kings' 1992-93 season, scoring crucial goals in both the regular season and playoffs. For his career, Taylor has compiled 421 goals and 626 assists for 1,047 points.

Imports

The Calgary Flame's Sergei Makarov is a veteran of the international hockey wars. He is a brilliant playmaker from Russia, where he was a regular Soviet All-Star selection. Three times he was selected Soviet Player of the Year and played on three Soviet Olympic teams resulting in two gold medals (1984, 1988). He also played in the 1981 Canada Cup. With the fall of the Soviet Union came freedom for Makarov, who quickly signed with Calgary for the 1989-90 season. The 31-year-old NHL rookie proceeded to stun the league, scoring 24 goals and 62 assists in winning the Calder Trophy. He added to his laurels in the next two years, becoming one of the star forwards in the NHL.

The Vancouver Canucks have struck gold with their Russian import. Pavel Bure (pronounced boo-RAY) is a fast and devious skater, equally capable of pinpoint shooting or passing. Born in Moscow in 1971, the left winger won the Soviet National League Rookie-of-the-Year in 1989. In 1991, Bure packed his bags and headed for the money and glamor of the NHL. Vancouver welcomed him with open arms. Bure returned the favor. In his first year with the league, he scored 34 goals and 26 assists in leading Vancouver to the Smythe Division regular season title. The NHL awarded Bure the Calder Trophy as the league's top rookie (two rookie awards in two leagues). His next year in the league was even better as he scored 60 goals and 50 assists for 110 points in 83 games as the Canucks finished first again in the Smythe Division.

New Faces

At no time has the NHL possessed so many great wingers, or so many young ones. Two of the best are on the team that seems to need them least.

Another international star, now playing for the Canucks, is Pavel Bure.

Even with superstar Mario Lemieux, the Pittsburgh Penguins can also boast two of the league's best wingers: Kevin Stevens and Czech import Jaromir Jagr. Stevens' best year to date was 1991-92 when he riddled opponents' nets with 54 goals while playing on the same line as Lemieux. Meanwhile, Jaromir Jagr, only 21 years old, is developing the kinds of moves usually reserved for hockey's legends. A one-man highlight film, Jagr is destined for greatness.

The Islanders also lay claim to two of the league's best: Ray Ferraro and Pierre Turgeon. In 1992-93 they not only enjoyed excellent regular seasons, but catapulted New York into the Conference finals, toppling mighty Pittsburgh before succumbing to Montreal.

Winnipeg's right wing Teemu Selanne was nothing if not a rookie sensation in 1992-93. Born in Helsinki, Finland, Selanne (pronounced SEH-lahn-nay) is both a deadly shot and a speed merchant. In his first year in the NHL he scored 76 goals and 56 assists for 132 points in 84 games. That tied Buffalo's talented right winger Alexander Mogilny for the most goals in the league, ranking fifth overall in total points. Not only did the young Finn walk away with the Calder Trophy as the league's most outstanding rookie, but he established a record for the most goals and points ever scored by a rookie in the NHL. With rookies like these, the reputation of the NHL hockey winger as an ice warrior is secure.

Most Goals, Single Season (Right Winger)

Names	Teams	Goals	Seasons
Brett Hull	St. Louis	86	1990-91
Brett Hull	St. Louis	72	1989-90
Jari Kurri	Edmonton, L.A.	71	1984-85
Brett Hull	St. Louis	70	1991-92
Mike Bossy	New York Islanders	69	1978-79
Jari Kurri	Edmonton, L.A.	68	1985-86
Mike Bossy	New York Islanders	69	1980-81

Most Goals, Single Season (Left Winger)

Names	Teams	Goals	Seasons
Steve Shutt	Montreal	60	1976-77
Bobby Hull	Chicago	58	1968-69
Michel Goulet	Quebec	57	1982-83
Charlie Simmer	L.A.	56	1979-80
Charlie Simmer	L.A.	56	1980-81
Michel Goulet	Quebec	56	1983-84

Most Goals, Career (Right Winger)

Names	Teams	Goals
Gordie Howe	Detroit, Hartford	801
Mike Bossy	NY Islanders	573
Guy LaFleur	NY Rangers	560
Maurice Richard	Montreal	544
Mike Gartner	Washington	544

Most Goals, Career (Left Winger)

Names	Teams	Goals
Bobby Hull	Chicago	610
Jim Bucky	Boston	556
Frank Mahovlich	Toronto, Detroit, Montreal	553
Michel Goulet	Quebec	509

Glossary

BACKHANDER. Any shot or pass made with the stick turned around.

BREAKAWAY. When a player has managed to get behind the opposing defense with the puck and is skating in all alone on the opposing goalie.

CHECKING. Defending against or guarding an opponent. On a line, a right wing checks the other team's left wing, and a left wing check's the opposing right wing.

CROSS-CHECKING. To hit an opponent with both hands on the stick and no part of the stick on the ice. Illegal and calls for a penalty.

DEKE. To feint or shift an opponent out of position.

FACE-OFF. The dropping of the puck between two opposing players to start play. Face-offs follow goals or other stoppages in action, and are to hockey what the jump ball is to basketball.

OFFSIDES. Called when an attacking player precedes the puck across the opponent's blue line.

PENALTY SHOT. A rare penalty when a player receives the chance to score one-on-one against the opposing goalie.

POWER PLAY. A manpower advantage resulting from a penalty to the opposing team.

SLAPSHOT. When a player winds up and slaps the puck with his stick, resulting in a hard, fast—but often erratic—shot.

STICK HANDLING. The art of controlling the puck with the stick.

Bibliography

Diamond, Dan & Joseph Romain. *Hockey Hall of Fame.* New York: Doubleday, 1988.

Diamond, Dan, ed. *National Hockey League 75th Anniversary Commemorative Book.* Toronto: McClellan & Stewart, 1993.

Hollander, Zander, ed. *The Complete Encyclopedia of Hockey.* Detroit: Visible Ink Press, 1993.

National Hockey League. *Official Guide & Record Book 1992-93.* Toronto: NHL Publications, 1993.

Sporting News. *Sporting News Complete Hockey Book 1993-94.* St. Louis, MO: The Sporting News Publishing Co., 1993.

Photo Credits

Index